Navigating Through Medicare

Dennis M. Postema

Navigating Through Medicare

Navigating Through Medicare. Copyright © 2013 The Retirement Institute/Dennis M. Postema. All rights reserved worldwide. Text cannot be distributed without prior written permission of the author, with the exception of brief, attributed quotations on Web and print media. For questions or permission of usage, please e-mail PostemaInsurance@netscape.net.

The information contained herein is for general purposes only. It is not meant to serve as an individual guide or suggestion. All information is based on Medicare and regulatory guidelines at the time of writing.

Third edition: August 2014

Discover other titles by Dennis M. Postema

http://NavigatingThroughMedicare.com

www.TheRetirementInstitute.org

Contents

About the Author 7

Using this Book 11

Chapter 1: Medicare Fundamentals 13

Understanding Medicare Parts 13

What Is Part A (Hospital Insurance) and What Does It Cover? 14

How Much Does Part A Cost? 15

How Do I Get Part A? 15

What Is Part B (Medical Insurance) and What Does It Cover? 17

How Much Does Part B Cost? 17

How Do I Get Part B? 17

What Is a Medicare Advantage Plan (Part C)? 19

Different Types of Medicare Advantage Plans 20

How Much Does a Medicare Advantage Plan Cost? 20

What Does a Medicare Advantage Plan Cover? 21

How to Join a Medicare Advantage Plan 21

A Few Extra Things You Should Know about Medicare Advantage Plans 22

Medicare Prescription Drug Coverage (Part D) 23

Ways to Get Medicare Drug Coverage 23

When Can You Join a Medicare Drug Plan? 24

How to Join a Medicare Drug Plan 24

Joining a Medicare Drug Plan May Affect Your Medicare Advantage Plan 25

How to Switch Your Medicare Drug Plan 25

What You Pay for Medicare Drug Coverage 26

Chapter 2: Medicare Supplement—Medigap 30

Medigap and Out-of-Pocket Expenses 31

Nine Things to Know about Medigap Policies 32

Insurance Plans that Aren't Medigap 33

Dropping Your Medigap Policy 33

Switching Medigap Policies 34

Plan F 40

Plan G 46

Cheaper Alternatives to Plans F and G 52

Plan Checklist 59

Medigap versus Medicare Advantage Plans 60

Medigap and Travel 66

Medigap Coverage Outside the U.S...66

Chapter 3: Open Enrollment and Guaranteed Issue 68

Understanding Open Enrollment...68

The Benefits of Open Enrollment *69*

What Happens During Open Enrollment... *70*

Understanding Guaranteed Issue Rights..74

Your Guaranteed Issue Rights *76*

Chapter 4: Budgeting for Medicare 80

Look at the Numbers and Assume the Worst 80

Making Adjustments...81

Finding Balance..82

Developing Alternatives...83

Chapter 5: Frequently Asked Questions 84

Chapter 6: Glossary... 96

About the Author

Dennis M. Postema, RFC, is a successful entrepreneur, best-selling author, speaker and registered financial consultant. He is the founder of MotivationandSuccess.com, StoriesofPerseverance.org and DaretoSucceed.net.

Dennis' dedication to his agents and clients has helped his business flourish and made him a 2012 recipient of the 10 Under 40 Award given by the Defiance Chamber of Commerce. He was also awarded the 2013 Distinguished Alumni Award from his alma mater, Northwest State Community College, for his success in the industry and community. His contribution to Jack Canfield's book, *Dare to Succeed*, earned him an Editor's Choice award.

Over the past 10 years, Dennis has taught clients, agents and associates how to find motivation and ascend psychological barriers to achieve success in all areas of their lives. Dennis' focus on helping clients, rather than simply selling them products, landed him on the cover of Agents Sales Journal (Senior Market Edition) in 2011.

Dennis's personal experience with tragedy, life-changing surgeries and health issues has given him a unique perspective on what it means to achieve success and what's really standing in the way of it. He channels that perspective into his series of educational and motivational books in the topics of finance, perseverance, success and business.

Disclaimer

All information provided in this book has been researched and is accurate and complete to the best of the author's knowledge. The author is not responsible for any errors or omissions, and there is no guarantee of completeness, accuracy or timeliness regarding the information provided throughout this book. You may use this information however you feel necessary, but you assume full responsibility for any potential loss that may occur from the use of this information.

Dennis M. Postema will not be liable for any direct, indirect, consequential, special, incidental or punitive damages or any other damages whatsoever. Under no circumstance will Dennis M. Postema, related partnerships, corporations or other direct relationships of the author be held liable to you or anyone else for any information relied upon by you from this book. You assume full risk and responsibility for how you use the information provided in this book.

All information in this book that was accurate at the time of publication may change at any time. Many sections were obtained from Medicare.gov per the Public Domain Dedication (found at http://www.medicare.gov/rss/Publicdomain.htm). Some content has been modified to make it more accessible. Changes in the market, laws or other circumstances that arise may cause these facts to change and the information provided throughout this book may not be assumed to be correct at all times. Individual environmental changes can cause the results in this book to vary at any time. All decisions made due to information provided in this book are the sole responsibility of the reader.

Using this Book

The first chapter of this book was written to give you a five-minute guide to Medicare. While it's not advisable to read only the first chapter, and then make decisions regarding Medicare coverage, it isn't impossible.

The next several sections were written to help break down the complex and confusing subject of Medicare, making it easier to understand and empowering you to make educated decisions. These are, perhaps, the most important pages because they give you the intangible confidence that not only helps you sleep at night knowing you made the right decisions for your retirement, but it also helps you avoid becoming the victim of a scam artist or greedy salesperson.

I believe Medicare can be the best health insurance on the planet provided you make the proper choices early. If you want the maximum amount of detailed information—beyond even what this book offers—go to medicare.gov where you can research the ins and outs of the system until your eyes drop out—something Medicare does, in fact, cover.

General Creighton Abrams once said, "When eating an elephant, take one bite at a time." Let's take his advice, and get started!

Chapter 1: Medicare Fundamentals

When you turn 65, whether you retire, stay working and/or leave your work-related health insurance, you go on Medicare. Your initial enrollment can begin when you turn 65 or when you sign up for Part B during the three months before and after your 65th birthday month. This gives you a seven-month window for initial enrollment. If you sign up for a Medicare Supplement plan, you have a six-month open enrollment period that starts the month you turn 65 and are enrolled in Part B.

Understanding Medicare Parts

There are fundamental building blocks—four basic parts—on which Medicare benefits are organized.

- Part A = Hospital Insurance
- Part B = Medical Insurance
- Part C = Medicare Advantage
- Part D = Prescriptions

What Is Part A (Hospital Insurance) and What Does It Cover?

Part A is hospital insurance that helps cover inpatient care in hospitals, skilled nursing facilities, hospice and home healthcare.

To find out if Part A covers something specific, visit the Medicare website. In general, Part A covers:

- Inpatient care in hospitals (such as critical access hospitals, inpatient rehabilitation facilities and long-term care hospitals)
- Inpatient care in a skilled nursing facility (not custodial or long-term care)
- Hospice care services
- Home healthcare services
- Inpatient care in a religious nonmedical healthcare institution

Note: Staying overnight in a hospital doesn't always mean you're an inpatient. For example, if you stay overnight for observation, Medicare may not cover it because you might not have been admitted. You're considered an inpatient the day a doctor formally admits you to a hospital with a doctor's order. Being an inpatient or an outpatient affects what you pay and whether you'll qualify for Part A coverage in a skilled nursing facility. Always ask if you're an inpatient or an outpatient. Read the Medicare handout, **"Are You a Hospital Inpatient or Outpatient? If You Have Medicare—Ask!"** for more information.

How Much Does Part A Cost?

Part A is the portion you've paid into through Medicare taxes during your working life, which means most people don't pay a Part A premium. This is called "premium-free Part A."

If you aren't eligible for premium-free Part A, you may be able to buy Part A if you meet one of these conditions:

- You're 65 or older, meet the citizenship or residency requirements and have (or are enrolling in) Part B.
- You're under 65, disabled and your premium-free Part A coverage ended because you returned to work. If you're under 65 and disabled, you can continue getting premium-free Part A for up to eight and a half (8.5) years after you return to work.

In most cases, if you choose to buy Part A, you must also have Part B and pay monthly premiums for both. If you have limited income and resources, your state may help you pay for Part A and/or Part B.

How Do I Get Part A?

Some individuals are automatically enrolled in Part A, such as those with ALS or who are receiving Social Security benefits. These folks will receive a Medicare card in the mail three months before they turn 65 or, for those who are disabled, during their 25th month of disability.

Individuals who still work and do not yet receive Social Security benefits can apply online or at their local Social Security office. Individuals with end-stage renal disease who are under 65 may also qualify and should contact Social Security to sign up.

What Is Part B (Medical Insurance) and What Does It Cover?

Part B helps cover medically necessary treatment such as doctors' services, outpatient care, durable medical equipment and home health services (for medically necessary assistance, not for activities of daily living). Part B also covers some preventive services. To find out if Part B covers something specific, visit the Medicare website. Part B covers two types of services:

- Medically necessary services—Services or supplies needed to diagnose or treat your medical condition and that meet accepted standards of medical practice
- Preventive services—Healthcare to prevent illness (i.e., flu) or detect it at an early stage when treatment is most likely to work best

Check your Medicare card to find out if you have Part B.

How Much Does Part B Cost?

If you have Part B, you pay a Part B premium each month. Most people pay the standard premium amount. Social Security contacts some people who must pay more depending on their income. If you don't sign up for Part B when you're first eligible, you may have to pay a late enrollment penalty.

How Do I Get Part B?

Retired individuals who get Social Security benefits, those with ALS and disabled individuals in their 25th month of disability are automatically signed up for Part B. Those who are still employed and qualified individuals under age 65 who have end-stage renal failure must apply online, by phone or at their local Social Security office.

What Is a Medicare Advantage Plan (Part C)?

A Medicare Advantage plan (like an HMO or PPO) is another health plan choice you may have as part of Medicare. Medicare Advantage plans, sometimes called "Part C" or "MA plans," are offered by private companies that have been approved by Medicare.

If you join a Medicare Advantage plan, it will provide all of your Part A (hospital insurance) and Part B (medical insurance) coverage. Medicare Advantage plans may offer extra coverage, such as vision, hearing, dental and/or health and wellness programs. It's important, however, to be careful as, often, this coverage sounds a lot more appealing than the benefits are actually worth. Most include Medicare prescription drug coverage (Part D).

Medicare pays a fixed amount for your care every month to the companies offering Medicare Advantage plans. These companies must follow rules set by Medicare. However, each Medicare Advantage plan can charge different out-of-pocket costs and have different rules for how you get services (i.e., whether you need a referral to see a specialist or if you can only visit doctors, facilities or suppliers that belong to the plan for nonemergency or non-urgent care). These rules can change each year. If you want to know where you stand at all times, a Medicare Supplement may be a more favorable option for you.

Different Types of Medicare Advantage Plans

There are four major types of Medicare Advantage plans to choose from. They are:

- Health Maintenance Organization (HMO) plans
- Preferred Provider Organization (PPO) plans
- Private Fee-for-Service (PFFS) plans
- Special Needs plans (SNP)

Other, less common types of Medicare Advantage plans may be available:

- HMO Point of Service (HMOPOS) Plans—An HMO plan that may allow you to get some services out-of-network for a higher cost
- Medical Savings Account (MSA) plans—Plans that combine a high deductible health plan with a bank account. Medicare deposits money into the account (usually less than the deductible). You can use the money to pay for your healthcare services during the year.

How Much Does a Medicare Advantage Plan Cost?

In addition to your Part B premium, you usually pay one monthly premium for the services included in your Medicare Advantage plan. Each Medicare Advantage plan can charge different out-of-pocket costs. Your out-of-pocket costs in a Medicare Advantage plan depend on:

- Whether the plan charges a monthly premium

- Whether the plan pays any of your monthly Part B premium
- Whether the plan has a yearly deductible or any additional deductibles
- How much you pay for each visit or service (copayments or coinsurance)
- The type of healthcare services you need and how often you get them
- Whether you follow the plan's rules (i.e., using network providers only)
- Whether you need extra benefits and if the plan charges for them
- The plan's yearly limit on your out-of-pocket costs for all medical services

What Does a Medicare Advantage Plan Cover?

In all types of Medicare Advantage plans, emergencies and urgent care are always covered. Medicare Advantage plans must cover all of the services original Medicare covers except hospice care. Original Medicare covers hospice care even if you're in a Medicare Advantage plan. Medicare Advantage plans aren't supplemental coverage; however, they may offer extra coverage such as vision, hearing, dental and/or health and wellness programs. Most include Medicare prescription drug coverage (Part D).

How to Join a Medicare Advantage Plan

Not all Medicare Advantage plans work the same, so before joining, take time to find and compare Medicare health plans in your area. Once you understand each plan's rules and costs and find one that works for you, you may be able to join via a paper application, calling the plan or enrolling on the plan's website. Medicare also has quality information to help you compare plans.

A Few Extra Things You Should Know about Medicare Advantage Plans

You can only join a plan at certain times during the year and, in most cases, your enrollment is good for one full year. As with original Medicare, you still have Medicare rights and protections, including the right to appeal.

- Check with the plan before you get a service to find out if it is covered and what your costs may be.
- You must follow plan rules. This may mean getting a referral to see a specialist or getting prior approval for certain procedures to avoid higher costs. Check with the plan.
- You can join a Medicare Advantage plan even if you have a preexisting condition, unless (during certain enrollment periods) that condition is end-stage renal disease.
- If you go to a doctor, facility or supplier that doesn't belong to the plan, your services may not be covered or your costs could be higher, depending on the type of Medicare Advantage plan you have.
- If the plan decides to stop participating in Medicare, you must join another Medicare health plan or return to original Medicare.

Medicare Prescription Drug Coverage (Part D)

Medicare offers prescription drug coverage to everyone with Medicare. If you decide not to join a Medicare drug plan when you're first eligible and you don't have other creditable prescription drug coverage, you'll likely pay a late enrollment penalty.

To get Medicare prescription drug coverage, you must join a plan run by an insurance company or other private company approved by Medicare. Each plan can vary in cost and drugs covered.

Ways to Get Medicare Drug Coverage

There are two ways to get Medicare prescription drug coverage:

1. Medicare prescription drug plans: These plans (sometimes called "PDPs") add drug coverage to original Medicare, some Medicare Cost plans, some Medicare Private Fee-for-Service (PFFS) plans, and Medicare Medical Savings Account (MSA) plans.

2. Medicare Advantage plans (like an HMO or PPO) or other Medicare health plans that offer Medicare prescription drug coverage: You get all of your Part A and Part B coverage and prescription drug coverage (Part D) through these plans. Medicare Advantage plans with prescription drug coverage are sometimes called "MA-PDs." You must have Part A and Part B to join a Medicare Advantage plan. Remember: if you get an Advantage plan with a built-in drug plan, it may not cover your drugs as completely as a

standalone plan with a formulary built around your exact prescriptions.

Both types of plans are called "Medicare drug plans." In either case, you must live in the service area of the Medicare drug plan you want to join.

When Can You Join a Medicare Drug Plan?

There are three occasions that introduce the opportunity to sign up for a Medicare drug plan:

- When you first get Medicare (initial enrollment period)
- During certain times each year (yearly enrollment periods)
- In special circumstances (special enrollment periods)

How to Join a Medicare Drug Plan

Once you choose a Medicare drug plan, you may be able to join by:

- Enrolling on the Medicare Plan Finder or on the plan's website
- Completing a paper application
- Calling the plan
- Calling 1-800-MEDICARE
- Enrolling online at Medicare.gov

When joining a Medicare drug plan, you give your Medicare number and the date your Part A and/or Part B coverage started. This information is on your Medicare card.

Joining a Medicare Drug Plan May Affect Your Medicare Advantage Plan

If your Medicare Advantage plan includes prescription drug coverage and you join a Medicare prescription drug plan, you'll be disenrolled from your Medicare Advantage plan and returned to original Medicare.

How to Switch Your Medicare Drug Plan

You can switch to a new Medicare drug plan simply by joining another drug plan during one of these aforementioned periods. You don't need to cancel your old Medicare drug plan or send them anything. Your old Medicare drug plan coverage will end when your new drug plan begins.

If you want to join a plan or switch plans, do so as soon as possible so you'll have your membership card when your coverage begins and you can get your prescriptions filled without delay. You should get a letter from your new Medicare drug plan telling you when your coverage begins.

Don't give personal information to representatives who call from plans you unless you're already a member of the plan.

What You Pay for Medicare Drug Coverage

Your actual drug plan costs vary depending on:

- The drugs you use
- The plan you choose
- Whether you go to a pharmacy in your plan's network
- If your drugs are on your plan's formulary
- Whether you get extra help paying your Part D costs

Look for specific Medicare drug plan costs, and then call the plans you're interested in to get more details. Or, go to Medicare.gov to compare various plans with your specific prescriptions.

If you have limited income and resources, check if you qualify for extra help to pay for Medicare prescription drug coverage. You may also be able to get help from your state.

Payments are made throughout the year in a Medicare drug plan:

- Monthly premium: Most drug plans charge a monthly fee in addition to the Part B premium. If you belong to a Medicare Advantage plan (like an HMO or PPO) or a Medicare Cost plan that includes Medicare prescription drug coverage, the plan's monthly premium may include an amount for prescription drug coverage.
- Yearly deductible: The amount you must pay each year for your prescriptions before your Medicare drug plan begins paying its share. Deductibles vary between Medicare drug

plans. No Medicare drug plan may have a deductible more than $310 in 2014. Some Medicare drug plans don't have a deductible but may have a higher premium as a result.

- Copayments or coinsurance: The amount you pay for each of your prescriptions after you have paid the deductible (if your plan has one). Some Medicare drug plans have different levels or "tiers" of coinsurance or copayments, with different costs for different types of drugs.

    - Coinsurance means you pay a percentage of the cost (for example, 25 percent) of the drug.
    - With a copayment, you pay a set amount (for example, $10) for all drugs on a tier. For example, you may pay a lower copayment for generic drugs than brand-name drugs.

- Coverage gap costs: Most Medicare drug plans have a coverage gap (also called the "donut hole"). This means there's a temporary limit on what the drug plan will cover for prescription medications.

Not everyone will enter the coverage gap. The coverage gap begins after you and your drug plan have spent a certain amount for covered medications. Also, people with Medicare who get extra help paying Part D costs won't enter the coverage gap.

Once you enter the coverage gap, you get a 52.5 percent manufacturer-paid discount on covered brand-name drugs. While you'll only pay the remaining 47.5 percent of the price for that brand-name drug, the entire price will count as out-of-pocket spending, which will help you get out of the coverage gap.

- Extra help costs: Many programs are available to help low-income seniors with medical expenses. Medicaid is one of the most popular. It's a joint program between the federal and state governments. The Medicare website has a full list of programs you can consult.
- Late-enrollment penalty: The late enrollment penalty for Part D varies depending on how long you went without creditable coverage for prescriptions. Generally, 1 percent of the national base beneficiary premium is multiplied by the number of months you were uncovered but eligible. In 2014, the national base beneficiary premium is $32.42.

Contact your drug plan, not Social Security, to have your premium deducted from your monthly Social Security payment. Your first deduction usually takes three months to start, and three months of premiums will likely be deducted at once.

Afterwards, only one premium will be deducted each month. You may also see a delay in premiums being withheld if you switch plans. If you want to stop premium deductions and get billed directly, contact your drug plan.

A small group—fewer than 5 percent of all people with Medicare—may pay a higher monthly premium for Part D coverage based on their income. This includes Part D coverage from a Medicare prescription drug plan, Medicare Advantage plan, or Medicare Cost plan including Medicare drug coverage.

If your modified adjusted gross income as reported on your IRS tax return from two years ago (the most recent tax return information provided to Social Security by the IRS) is above a certain limit, you'll pay an extra amount in addition to your plan premium. Usually, the extra amount is deducted from your Social Security check. For more details, see Social Security's brochure, *Medicare Premiums: Rules for Higher Income Beneficiaries*. Contact Social Security if you have to pay an extra amount and you disagree (for example, you have a life event that lowers your income).

Chapter 2: Medicare Supplement—Medigap

A Medicare supplement (Medigap) insurance, sold by private companies, helps pay some of the healthcare costs original Medicare doesn't cover, such as copayments, coinsurance and deductibles.

Some Medigap policies also offer coverage for services original Medicare doesn't cover, like medical care when traveling outside the U.S. If you have original Medicare and you buy a Medigap policy, Medicare pays its share of the Medicare-approved amount for covered healthcare costs. Then, your Medigap policy pays its share.

A Medigap policy differs from a Medicare Advantage plan. Those plans are ways to get Medicare benefits, while a Medigap policy only supplements your original Medicare benefits.

One of the greatest things about Medigap policies isn't that they help reduce the potential burden of medical costs on seniors and the disabled, it's that those who use it are very satisfied. A 2012 survey of Medigap satisfaction levels among seniors, aged 65 and older, conducted by AmericanViewpoint showed that 90 percent of all Medigap policyholders were happy with their coverage. In addition, 59 percent of those who were satisfied with Medicare overall actually considered themselves to be very satisfied and 63 percent were very satisfied with Medigap. This showed that it is one of the most popular ways to structure a postretirement medical care program.

While quality of treatment is very important to determining satisfaction levels, value is an even greater indicator. Seventy-nine percent of Medigap enrollees said their policy provided good to excellent value for the premiums they pay in.

However, the biggest recommendation given by these satisfied seniors was they would happily, in nine out of 10 cases, recommend Medigap coverage to a friend or family member.

Medigap and Out-of-Pocket Expenses

One may think seniors with Medigap policies, which may have deductibles, would be overly concerned about the amount of out-of-pocket expenses they could face. However, the survey by AmericanViewpoint says differently. According to the survey, 52 percent of Medigap enrollees did not worry at all about out-of-pocket expenses before going to the doctor or hospital. In fact, more enrollees were worried about the possibility of Medigap coverage being eliminated than they were about increases in out-of-pocket costs—that's how much they loved this coverage.

Nine Things to Know about Medigap Policies

1. To have a Medigap policy, you must have Medicare Part A and Part B.

2. If you have a Medicare Advantage plan, you can apply for a Medigap policy, but make sure you can leave the Medicare Advantage plan before your Medigap policy begins. You can't have both in force at the same time.

3. You pay the private insurance company a monthly premium for your Medigap policy in addition to the monthly Part B premium you pay to Medicare.

4. A Medigap policy only covers one person. If you and your spouse both want Medigap coverage, you each have to buy separate policies. Medicare Advantage works the same way.

5. You can buy a Medigap policy from any insurance company that is licensed in your state to sell one.

6. Any standardized Medigap policy is guaranteed renewable, even if you have health problems. Therefore, the insurance company can't cancel your Medigap policy as long as you pay the premium.

7. Some Medigap policies sold in the past cover prescription drugs, but Medigap policies sold after January 1, 2006, aren't allowed to include prescription

drug coverage. If you want prescription drug coverage, you can join a Medicare prescription drug plan (Part D).

8. It's illegal for anyone to sell you a Medigap policy if you have a Medicare Medical Savings Account (MSA) plan.

9. Medigap policies don't cover everything. For example, they generally don't cover long-term care, vision or dental care, hearing aids, eyeglasses or private-duty nursing.

Insurance Plans that Aren't Medigap
Some types of insurance aren't Medigap plans, including:

- Medicare Advantage plans (like an HMO, PPO or Private Fee-for-Service plan)
- Medicare prescription drug plans
- Medicaid
- Employer or union plans, including the Federal Employees Health Benefits Program (FEHBP)
- TRICARE
- Veterans' benefits
- Long-term care insurance policies
- Indian Health Service, Tribal, and Urban Indian Health plans

Dropping Your Medigap Policy
If you decide to drop the entire Medigap policy, you need to be careful about the timing. For example, you may want a

completely different Medigap policy or decide to switch to a Medicare Advantage plan offering prescription drug coverage.

If you drop your entire drug plan and/or the drug coverage wasn't creditable or you go more than 63 days before your new prescription coverage begins, you must pay a late enrollment penalty for your Medicare prescription drug plan Drug plans and Medigap are separate coverages that have nothing to do with each other, but with a Medicare Advantage plan, you can streamline your coverage by choosing one with built-in drug coverage. If you get confused at all, don't just take a guess. Talk to someone who specializes in all of the plans so you can get the exact coverage you want and need.

Switching Medigap Policies

You have 30 days to decide if you want to keep a new Medigap policy. It's called your "free look period" and starts when you get your new Medigap policy. You'll need to request an effective date at least one month out so you don't pay both premiums for one month. For example, if it's March 3, you want to make the new policy effective date no earlier than April 1 so you have time to get your new policy, read it and cancel the old one, thus preventing having two policies in force at once.

Don't cancel your first Medigap policy until you've decided to keep the second Medigap policy. On the application for the new Medigap policy, you must promise to cancel your first policy.

There are four reasons you may want to switch Medigap policies:

- You're paying for benefits you don't need.

- You need more benefits than you needed before.

- Your current Medigap policy has the right benefits, but you want to change insurance companies.

- Your current Medigap policy has the right benefits, but you want to find a less expensive policy that features the exact same coverage.

In most cases, you have the right to switch Medigap policies at any time, if you qualify. In other words, you don't have to wait a certain length of time after buying your first Medigap policy before you can switch to a different one.

If you have a Medigap policy dated prior to 1992, you don't have to switch, but if you choose to buy a new Medigap policy, you must give up your old policy. Once you cancel the policy, you can't get it back, and it can no longer be sold because it isn't a standardized policy.

If you bought your policy before 2010, it may offer coverage that isn't available in a newer policy, which is an important point to consider before taking on a new policy. If you bought your policy before 1992, your policy might not be a guaranteed renewable policy and may have a bigger premium increase than newer, standardized Medigap policies currently being sold.

Also, the Medigap insurance company may be able to make you wait up to six months for coverage of preexisting conditions. The number of months you've had your current Medigap policy must be subtracted from the time you must wait before your new

Medigap policy covers your preexisting condition; however, if you've had your old policy for six months or more, the new insurance company can't exclude your preexisting condition. Generally, most companies today either issue the policy with no preexisting exclusions or opt not to issue the policies at all so there is less confusion.

On the next few pages, we'll show you all the different Medicare supplement plans and benefits available. These plans are, by law, the exact same no matter which insurer you choose. The only difference is in the premium. Don't be fooled into thinking you can't shop around—you *can* change your supplement policy at any time throughout the year, as long as your health qualifies.

Benefit Chart of Medicare Supplement Plans/Outline of Coverage

This chart shows the benefits included in each of the standard Medicare supplement plans. Every company must make "Plan A" available. Some plans may not be available in your state. Plans E, H, I and J are no longer available for sale.

BASIC BENEFITS

Hospitalization: Part A coinsurance plus coverage for 365 additional days after Medicare benefits end

Medical Expenses: Part B coinsurance (generally 20 percent of Medicare-approved expenses) or copayments for hospital outpatient services; Plans K, L and N require insureds to pay a portion of Part B coinsurance or copayments

Blood: First three pints of blood each year

Hospice: Part A coinsurance

* Plan F also offers a high-deductible plan. If you choose this option, you must pay for Medicare-covered costs up to the deductible amount of $2,140 (in 2014) before your Medigap plan pays anything.

** After you meet your out-of-pocket yearly limit and your yearly Part B deductible, the Medigap plan pays 100 percent of covered services for the rest of the calendar year.

*** Plan N pays 100 percent of the Part B coinsurance, except for a copayment of up to $20 for some office visits and up to a $50 copayment for emergency room visits that don't result in inpatient admission.

Navigating Through Medicare

A	B	C	D	F F*	G
Basic Benefits, including 100% of Part B coinsurance	Basic Benefits, including 100% of Part B coinsurance	Basic Benefits, including 100% of Part B coinsurance	Basic Benefits, including 100% of Part B coinsurance	Basic Benefits, including 100% of Part B coinsurance*	Basic Benefits, including 100% of Part B coinsurance
		Skilled Nursing Facility Coinsurance	Skilled Nursing Facility Coinsurance	Skilled Nursing Facility Coinsurance	Skilled Nursing Facility Coinsurance
	Part A Deductible	Part A Deductible	Part A Deductible	Part A Deductible	Part A Deductible
		Part B Deductible		Part B Deductible	
				Part B Excess (100%)	Part B Excess (100%)
		Foreign Travel Emergency	Foreign Travel Emergency	Foreign Travel Emergency	Foreign Travel Emergency

Navigating Through Medicare

K	L	M	N
Hospitalization and preventive care paid at 100%; other basic benefits paid at 50%	Hospitalization and preventive care paid at 100%; other basic benefits paid at 75%	Basic Benefits, including 100% of Part B coinsurance	Basic Benefits, including 100% of Part B coinsurance except up to $20 copayment for office visit & up to $50 copayment for ER
50% Skilled Nursing Facility Coinsurance	75% Skilled Nursing Facility Coinsurance	Skilled Nursing Facility Coinsurance	Skilled Nursing Facility Coinsurance
50% Part A Deductible	75% Part A Deductible	50% Part A Deductible	Part A Deductible
Out-of-pocket limit for Plan K is $4,620; paid at 100% after limit reached	Out-of-pocket limit for Plan L is $2,310; paid at 100% after limit reached	Foreign Travel Emergency	Foreign Travel Emergency

It may seem like a lot, but don't become overwhelmed by the separate plans and choices. It's actually much easier than you think to pick a plan that offers the best benefits and value—and in my opinion, that's by sticking with the three plans highlighted in gray.

There may be a few differences among these three plans, so, to narrow it down, I suggest conducting further research based on your zip code.

Let's look at these three in detail, starting with Plan F.

Plan F

This is the most common plan and rightfully so as you can clearly see on the last page it has the most benefits. Most of America has this plan. If you like to know where you stand at all times, this is the plan for you. Plan F has no surprises and, as long as you apply during your open enrollment period, you won't be subject to medical approval. Now, let's take a look at a detailed breakdown on the next five pages. You will notice that, through the whole spate of Plan F offerings, the out-of-pocket cost to you is little to nothing—which helps make this plan so popular.

Plan F

Medicare (Part A) - Hospital Services - Per Benefit Period

*A benefit period begins on the first day you receive service as an inpatient in a hospital and ends after you have been out of the hospital and have not received skilled care in any other facility for 60 days in a row.

SERVICES	MEDICARE PAYS	PLAN PAYS	YOU PAY
HOSPITALIZATION* Semiprivate room and board, general nursing and miscellaneous services and supplies			
First 60 days	All but $1,184	$1,184 (Part A deductible)	$0
61st thru 90th day	All but $296 per day	$296 per day	$0
91st day and after: While using 60 lifetime reserve days	All but $592 per day	$592 per day	$0
Once lifetime reserve days are used: Additional 365 days	$0	100% of Medicare eligible expenses	$0**
Beyond additional 365 days	$0	$0	All costs

Navigating Through Medicare

SERVICES	MEDICARE PAYS	PLAN PAYS	YOU PAY
SKILLED NURSING FACILITY CARE* You must meet Medicare's requirements, including having been in a hospital for at least three (3) days and entered a Medicare-approved facility within 30 days after leaving hospital			
First 20 days	All approved amounts	$0	$0
21st thru 100th day	All but $148 a day	Up to $148 a day	$0
101st day and after	$0	$0	All costs
BLOOD: First three (3) pints	$0	3 pints	$0
Additional amounts	100%	$0	$0
HOSPICE CARE You must meet Medicare's requirements, including a doctor's certification of terminal illness	All but very limited copayment/coinsurance for outpatient drugs and inpatient respite care	Medicare copayment/coinsurance	$0

NOTICE: When your Medicare Part A hospital benefits are exhausted, the Plan stands in the place of Medicare and pays whatever amount Medicare would have paid for up to an additional 365 days as provided in the policy's "Core Benefits." During this time, the hospital is prohibited from billing you for the balance based on any difference between its billed charges and the amount Medicare would have paid.

Navigating Through Medicare

Plan F (continued)

Medicare (Part B) - Medical Services - Per Calendar Year

*Once you have been billed $140 of Medicare-approved amounts for covered services (which are noted with an asterisk), your Part B deductible is met for the calendar year.

SERVICES	MEDICARE PAYS	PLAN PAYS	YOU PAY
MEDICAL EXPENSES **IN OR OUT OF THE HOSPITAL AND OUTPATIENT HOSPITAL TREATMENT**, such as physician's services, inpatient and outpatient medical and surgical services and supplies, physical and speech therapy, diagnostic tests, durable medical equipment			
First $147 of Medicare-approved amounts*	$0	$147 (Part B deductible)	$0
Remainder of Medicare-approved amounts	Generally 80%	Generally 20%	$0
Part B Excess Charges (above Medicare-approved amounts)	$0	100%	$0
BLOOD: First three (3) pints	$0	All costs	$0

43

Navigating Through Medicare

SERVICES	MEDICARE PAYS	PLAN PAYS	YOU PAY
Next $147 of Medicare-approved amounts*	$0	$147 (Part B deductible)	$0
Remainder of Medicare-approved amounts	80%	20%	$0
CLINICAL LABORATORY SERVICES TESTS FOR DIAGNOSTIC SERVICES	100%	$0	$0

PARTS A & B

SERVICES	MEDICARE PAYS	PLAN PAYS	YOU PAY
HOME HEALTHCARE MEDICARE-APPROVED SERVICES - Medically necessary skilled care services and medical supplies	100%	$0	$0
Durable medical equipment - first $147 of Medicare-approved amounts*	$0	$147 (Part B deductible)	$0
Remainder of Medicare-approved amounts	80%	20%	$0

44

Navigating Through Medicare

SERVICES	MEDICARE PAYS	PLAN PAYS	YOU PAY
FOREIGN TRAVEL **NOT COVERED BY MEDICARE** Medically necessary emergency care services beginning during first 60 days of each trip outside U.S.	$0		
First $250 each calendar year	$0	$0	$250
Remainder of charges	$0	80% to a lifetime maximum benefit of $50,000	20% and amounts over the $50,000 lifetime maximum

Plan G

While Plan F is very well liked, Plan G is a great alternative that's gaining popularity. Between Plan F and Plan G, there is one major difference: the deductible for Part B, present with Plan G but not with Plan F. However, there is another benefit in Plan G that makes up for the deductible, and that is found in the premiums, which are less likely to increase exponentially from year to year.

You see, Plan G requires medical underwriting for all applicants except during open enrollment. Therefore, those with medical conditions costly for insurers to cover are often turned down. With Plan G, the insurance company actuaries can maintain a good handle on what the anticipating cost of claims will be which allows them to apply less expensive premiums and maintain a steady rise in premium renewal costs.

Plan G is the exact same as Plan F, except you are required to pay your own Medicare Part B deductible of $147 in 2014.

If this sounds like too many words to you, let's break it down even more. With Plan G, you will save money. Period. Therefore, for most of my clients—those who will qualify based on their relative good health—I generally suggest Plan G. Let's take a look at the plan in detail on the next few pages.

Plan G

Medicare (Part A) - Hospital Services - Per Benefit Period

*A benefit period begins on the first day you receive service as an inpatient in a hospital and ends after you have been out of the hospital and have not received skilled care in any other facility for 60 consecutive days.

SERVICES	MEDICARE PAYS	PLAN PAYS	YOU PAY
HOSPITALIZATION* Semiprivate room and board, general nursing and miscellaneous services and supplies			
First 60 days	All but $1,184	$1,184 (Part A deductible)	$0
61st thru 90th day	All but $296 a day	$296 a day	$0
91st day and after: - While using 60 lifetime reserve days	All but $592 a day	$592 a day	$0
Once lifetime reserve days are used: - Additional 365 days	$0	100% of Medicare eligible expenses	$0**
-Beyond additional 365 days	$0	$0	All costs

Navigating Through Medicare

SERVICES	MEDICARE PAYS	PLAN PAYS	YOU PAY
SKILLED NURSING FACILITY CARE* You must meet Medicare's requirements, including having been in a hospital for at least three days and entered a Medicare-approved facility within 30 days after leaving hospital			
First 20 days	All approved amounts	$0	$0
21st thru 100th day	All but $148 a day	Up to $148 a day	$0
101st day and after	$0	$0	All costs
BLOOD: First three (3) pints	$0	3 pints	$0
Additional amounts	100%	$0	$0
HOSPICE CARE You must meet Medicare's requirements, including a doctor's certification of terminal illness	All but very limited copayment/coinsurance for outpatient drugs and inpatient respite care	Medicare copayment/coinsurance	$0

**NOTICE: When Medicare Part A hospital benefits are exhausted, the Plan pays what Medicare would've paid up to an added 365 days per the policy's "Core Benefits." During this time, the hospital is prohibited from billing for the balance based on any difference between its billed charges and the amount Medicare would have paid.

Plan G (continued)

Medicare (Part B) - Medical Services - Per Calendar Year

*Once you have been billed $140 of Medicare-approved amounts for covered services (which are noted with an asterisk), your Part B deductible is met for the calendar year.

SERVICES	MEDICARE PAYS	PLAN PAYS	YOU PAY
MEDICAL EXPENSES IN OR OUT OF THE HOSPITAL AND OUTPATIENT HOSPITAL TREATMENT, such as physician's services, inpatient and outpatient medical and surgical services and supplies, physical and speech therapy, diagnostic tests, durable medical equipment			
First $147 of Medicare-approved amounts*	$0	$0	$147 (Part B deductible)
Remainder of Medicare-approved amounts	Generally 80%	Generally 20%	$0
Part B Excess Charges (above Medicare-approved amounts)	$0	100%	$0
BLOOD: First three (3) pints	$0	All costs	$0

Navigating Through Medicare

SERVICES	MEDICARE PAYS	PLAN PAYS	YOU PAY
Next $147 of Medicare-approved amounts*	$0	$0	$147 (Part B deductible)
Remainder of Medicare-approved amounts	80%	20%	$0
CLINICAL LABORATORY SERVICES Tests for diagnostic services	100%	$0	$0

Part A & B

SERVICES	MEDICARE PAYS	PLAN PAYS	YOU PAY
HOME HEALTHCARE MEDICARE-APPROVED SERVICES - Medically necessary skilled care services and medical supplies	100%	$0	$0
Durable medical equipment: First $147 of Medicare-approved amounts*	$0	$0	$147 (Part B deductible)
Remainder of Medicare-approved amounts	80%	20%	$0

*Once you have been billed $140 of Medicare-approved amounts for covered services (which are noted with an asterisk), your Part B deductible is met for the calendar year.

Plan G (continued)

OTHER BENEFITS - NOT COVERED BY MEDICARE

SERVICES	MEDICARE PAYS	PLAN PAYS	YOU PAY
FOREIGN TRAVEL NOT COVERED BY MEDICARE Medically necessary emergency care services beginning during first 60 days of each trip outside U.S.			
First $250 each calendar year	$0	$0	$250
Remainder of charges	$0	80% to a lifetime maximum benefit of $50,000	20% and amounts over the $50,000 lifetime maximum

Cheaper Alternatives to Plans F and G

We've discussed Plans F and G in great detail, but there are alternatives to these two plans that can be less expensive without sacrificing too many benefits. For seniors with a fixed income, these alternatives could be just the ticket.

The plans we're about to cover are especially good if you like the lower premiums of a Medicare Advantage plan and prefer the comfort of knowing the Medicare supplement is standardized.

High-Deductible Plan F

First is High-Deductible Plan F. It has all the benefits of regular Plan F, but with a higher deductible, it allows you more control over your total spending. The higher deductible gives you a lower premium since it makes you more responsible for paying the cost of your care initially—at least until you've spent the total amount of your deductible. Best of all, you can decide when to spend that deductible by carefully choosing when to see a doctor.

Plan N

The second alternative I'd like to mention is Plan N. As with High-Deductible Plan F, Plan N allows you more control by giving you a low premium and option for a high deductible as well as copayments, which further spreads the responsibility for payment between you and your insurer.

Plan N has many of the same benefits as Plan F. However, it cuts your premiums through affordable, reasonable copayments, the deductible, and by leaving you responsible for excess charges that nonparticipating medical providers are permitted to charge (capped at 15 percent above Medicare's payment). This fee is also totally avoidable if you choose a participating medical facility instead of a nonparticipating one, but it does allow you the ever-important freedom of choice.

On the next few pages, we'll take a close look at what Plan N has to offer.

Navigating Through Medicare

Plan N

Medicare (Part A) - Hospital Services - Per Benefit Period

*A benefit period begins on the first day you receive service as an inpatient in a hospital and ends after you have been out of the hospital and have not received skilled care in any other facility for 60 consecutive days.

SERVICES	MEDICARE PAYS	PLAN PAYS	YOU PAY
HOSPITALIZATION* Semiprivate room and board, general nursing and miscellaneous services and supplies			
First 60 days	All but $1,184	$1,184 (Part A deductible)	$0
61st thru 90th day	All but $296 a day	$296 a day	$0
91st day and after: - While using 60 lifetime reserve days	All but $592 a day	$592 a day	$0
Once lifetime reserve days are used: - Additional 365 days	$0	100% of Medicare eligible expenses	$0**
- Beyond additional 365 days	$0	$0	All costs

Navigating Through Medicare

SERVICES	MEDICARE PAYS	PLAN PAYS	YOU PAY
SKILLED NURSING FACILITY CARE* You must meet Medicare's requirements, including having been in a hospital for at least three days and entered a Medicare-approved facility within 30 days after leaving the hospital.			
First 20 days	All approved amounts	$0	$0
21st thru 100th day	All but $148 a day	Up to $148 a day	$0
101st day and after	$0	$0	All costs
BLOOD: First three (3) pints	$0	3 pints	$0
Additional amounts	100%	$0	$0
HOSPICE CARE You must meet Medicare's requirements, including a doctor's certification of terminal illness	All but very limited copayment/coinsurance for outpatient drugs and inpatient respite care	Medicare copayment/coinsurance	$0

**NOTICE: When your Medicare Part A hospital benefits are exhausted, the Plan stands in the place of Medicare and pays whatever amount Medicare would have paid for up to an additional 365 days as provided in the policy's "Core Benefits." During this time, the hospital is prohibited from billing you for the balance based on any difference between its billed charges and the amount Medicare would have paid.

Medicare (Part B) - Medical Services - Per Calendar Year

*Once you have been billed $147 of Medicare-approved amounts for covered services (which are noted with an asterisk), your Part B deductible is met for the calendar year.

SERVICES	MEDICARE PAYS	PLAN PAYS	YOU PAY
MEDICAL EXPENSES In or out of the hospital and outpatient treatment, such as physician's services, inpatient and outpatient medical and surgical services and supplies, physical and speech therapy, diagnostic tests, durable medical equipment			
First $147 of Medicare-approved amounts*	$0	$0	$147 (Part B deductible)

Navigating Through Medicare

SERVICES	MEDICARE PAYS	PLAN PAYS	YOU PAY
Remainder of Medicare-approved amounts	Generally 80%	Balance, other than up to $20 per office visit and up to $50 per ER visit. The copayment of up to $50 is waived if the insured is admitted to any hospital and the emergency visit is covered as a Medicare Part A expense.	Up to $20 per office visit and up to $50 per ER visit. The copayment of up to $50 is waived if the insured is admitted to any hospital and the emergency visit is covered as a Medicare Part A expense.
Part B Excess Charges (above Medicare-approved amounts)	$0	$0	All costs
BLOOD: First three (3) pints	$0	All costs	$0
Next $147 of Medicare-approved amounts*	$0	$0	$147 (Part B deductible)
Remainder of Medicare-approved amounts	80%	20%	$0
CLINICAL LABORATORY SERVICES Tests for diagnostic services	100%	$0	$0

PARTS A & B

SERVICES	MEDICARE PAYS	PLAN PAYS	YOU PAY
HOME HEALTHCARE Medicare-approved services - Medically necessary skilled care services and medical supplies	100%	$0	$0
Durable medical equipment - first $147 of Medicare-approved amounts*	$0	$0	$147 (Part B deductible)
Remainder of Medicare-approved amounts	80%	20%	$0
FOREIGN TRAVEL NOT COVERED BY MEDICARE Medically necessary emergency care services beginning during first 60 days of each trip outside U.S.			
First $250 each calendar year	$0	$0	$250
Remainder of charges	$0	80% to a lifetime maximum benefit of $50,000	20% and amounts over the $50,000 lifetime maximum

58

Navigating Through Medicare

Plan Checklist

To help determine which plan is best suited to your needs, answer the questions below.

1 Are you in good health?	Yes	No
2 Do you have enough saved to handle deductibles and copayments?	Yes	No
3 Do you plan to do any foreign travel, including to Mexico or Canada?	Yes	No
4 Do you need to maintain strict control over your premiums?	Yes	No
5 Can you restrict your doctor visits each year?	Yes	No
6 Do you have preexisting conditions?	Yes	No
7 Are low premiums more important than high deductibles?	Yes	No

If you answered "Yes" to question 1, then underwritten plans such as Plan G might be a good choice.

If you answered "No" to question 2, then Plan G or Plan F may fit your needs.

If you answered "Yes" to question 3, then plans such as F, F High-Deductible, G or N may be perfect options.

If you answered "Yes" to question 1 and 4, Plan G might be a good choice.

If you answered "Yes" to questions 1, 3 and 5, then Plan G may be a perfect fit.

If you answered "Yes" to question 7, then High-Deductible Plan F might be a good choice.

Medigap versus Medicare Advantage Plans

It's not always easy to decide between a Medigap plan or a Medicare Advantage plan. The main difference between is that Medigap plans, as official Medicare supplements, are standardized. Medicare Advantage plans, however, can offer different benefits than Medigap plans and have minimum requirements for benefits.

One of the most persuasive points for many seniors choosing between Medigap and Medicare Advantage plans is that Medigap, being standardized across the board, makes it easy to always know where you stand. The companies offering Medicare Advantage plans, on the other hand, can change the plan coverage, cost and providers year after year—which puts you at their mercy.

On the following pages is a detailed breakdown of the two.

Navigating Through Medicare

Medicare Advantage vs. Medigap Comparison Chart

Comparison	Medicare Advantage	Medicare Supplement
	Source: Oregon.gov DCBS SHIBA	
Eligibility	Must have Parts A and B, and live in service area. Takes all applicants except those with end-stage renal disease (some exceptions).	Must have Parts A and B. Usually companies may deny based on health qualifications, but must accept all applicants of all ages during Medigap open enrollment and guaranteed issue periods.
Costs: (premium, copay, coinsurance, out-of-pocket max)	All plan members pay same premium regardless of age, gender or health. Cost sharing (copays) must be paid for most medical services. Many plans have an out-of-pocket annual maximum.	Premium varies with gender and health and increases with age. Companies may underwrite (add to premium). Generally, no copay costs at time of service. No out-of-pocket maximum.

Navigating Through Medicare

Comparison	Medicare Advantage	Medicare Supplement
Provider choice and availability (Always ask your providers what insurance they accept!)	**HMOs** and **PPOs** maintain provider network; they must have available providers to accept new members. **PFFS** has no provider network; it may be hard to find providers who accept it. **HMO:** Generally covers in-network only. Referrals may be required for specialist visits. **PPO:** Covers out of network, but costs may be higher. No referrals required.	**No network:** Go to any provider that accepts Medicare. No referrals required for specialist visits. May be hard to find providers accepting original Medicare. May be used for treatments at major medical facilities, such as Mayo Clinics, OHSU, etc.
Prescription drug coverage	If you want Rx coverage, you must enroll in the included Rx coverage	Not included. If you want Rx coverage, you may enroll in any standalone (PDP)

Navigating Through Medicare

Comparison	Medicare Advantage	Medicare Supplement
(Be sure your choice covers your Rx!)	when choosing an **HMO** or **PPO** (VA-eligible excepted). With **PFFS**, you may choose either the plan's Rx coverage, if offered, or a standalone PDP.	plan available.
Renewable?	No, benefits may change yearly. However, you usually remain in a plan unless you disenroll at election times.	Yes, guaranteed renewable as long as you pay the premium and the application was correct. Benefits never change. No election season for Medigaps.
Extras?	Some plans include routine dental, vision or physicals. Some offer an additional alternative medicine	Covers same as original Medicare. No routine dental, vision or physicals; no

Navigating Through Medicare

Comparison	Medicare Advantage	Medicare Supplement
Whom may it best fit?	package. Network plans may be good for people who otherwise can't find a Medicare provider. May save money unless you need frequent appointments or treatments. Has a packaged plan that may simplify choices.	alternative medicine. Good for travelers or "snow birds." May save money for people needing high-cost or frequent care. Customize elements of your Medicare picture—choose doctors and drug plan.

Navigating Through Medicare

Comparison	Medicare Advantage	Medicare Supplement
How to comparison shop: Use pages in Guide (and/or call SHIBA!)	Plans are not standardized—use comparison pages in this Guide or at www.medicare.gov. Plans are regulated by Medicare/CMS; sales agents are licensed by OID.	Because Medigaps are standardized, price and customer service are the only difference. Call a few competitively priced plans.

Medigap and Travel

According to Medicare.gov, some Medigap policies offer additional coverage for healthcare services or supplies that can be obtained outside the U.S. The website states:

Standard Medigap Plans C, D, F, G, M and N provide foreign travel emergency healthcare coverage when traveling outside the U.S.

Plans E, H, I and J are no longer for sale, but if you bought one before June 1, 2010, you may keep it. All of these plans also provide foreign travel emergency healthcare coverage when you travel outside the U.S.

Medigap Coverage Outside the U.S.

Many seniors look forward to their retirement years as the perfect time to explore the world. Without the constraints of a job, it really is the best time to travel—but your Medigap plan may not offer the same coverage outside the U.S. as it does within its borders. Thus, it is important to talk to your plan provider before leaving so you can find out whether you need to supplement your coverage while abroad.

The Medicare.gov website offers the following guidelines for overseas medical coverage:

Medigap Plans C, D, E, F, G, H, I, J, M and N pay 80 percent of the billed charges for certain medically necessary emergency care outside the U.S. after a $250 deductible is met for the year. These Medigap policies cover foreign travel emergency care if it begins during the first 60 days of your trip, and if Medicare doesn't otherwise cover the care.

Foreign travel emergency coverage with Medigap policies has a lifetime limit of $50,000.

Chapter 3: Open Enrollment and Guaranteed Issue

Open enrollment can be a confusing term because, in the world of Medigap, it means two different things.

Understanding Open Enrollment

First, there's your personal open enrollment period—which is the best time for you to secure a Medigap policy. Your personal open enrollment occurs only once in your lifetime. It happens during the six months after you enroll in Medicare Part B. The six-month term begins the very same month you enroll, which generally occurs after you reach age 65 and are accepted into the Medicare program.

Medicare open enrollment is between October 15 and December 7 each year. If you miss your open enrollment for a Medigap or Medicare Supplement plan, you don't get it back. With Medicare Advantage plans, on the other hand, you can change the plan each year without qualifying, unless you have end-stage renal disease.

While your personal enrollment period might not begin until you enroll in Medicare Part B, it may be in your best interests to apply for Medigap early if you have coverage scheduled to end once you hit age 65. By applying early, you can help ensure there are no gaps in your coverage.

The Benefits of Open Enrollment

So, why is open enrollment so important? You have certain rights during this period that you don't otherwise have. Mainly, you cannot be denied a Medigap policy for health reasons during your personal open enrollment. If you have preexisting conditions*, this is an extremely important benefit. In addition, an insurer cannot charge you more during open enrollment even if you are a tobacco user.

When applying outside of open enrollment, a Medigap insurer cannot delay the start of coverage, although they can build in a temporary exclusion of up to six months for a preexisting condition*. If they do so, your policy will only provide coverage for medical treatment unrelated to that temporarily excluded condition.

In some cases, having continuous coverage before the Medigap policy is issued can reduce or remove any preexisting condition exclusion. It has to be creditable coverage (check with Medicare to determine if your plan meets their definition of "creditable") and there must not have been a break in coverage longer than 63 days.

*Preexisting conditions are defined as health problems that have been diagnosed or treated within the six months prior to the issuance of the Medigap policy. However, if there are any preexisting conditions, most companies will wait until those are healed and recovered from before insuring you. Some carriers won't even issue a policy if you have any preexisting conditions.

What Happens During Open Enrollment

If you apply for a Medicare Advantage plan during annual open enrollment, companies have no underwriting standards to meet, other than you cannot have been diagnosed with end-stage renal disease.

If you apply during Medicare's open enrollment, however, Medigap insurance companies are generally allowed to medically underwrite your policy. Therefore, they can decide whether or not to accept your application based on your answers to certain health questions. However, if you apply during your personal open enrollment period, you can buy any Medigap policy the company sells, even if you have health problems, for the same price as people with perfect health.

As we mentioned in the last section, unless you enroll during your personal open enrollment period, there's no guarantee an insurance company will issue a Medigap policy to you, and there's no guarantee you will get the same premium as others.

However, there are a few additional circumstances that could allow you the benefit of a guaranteed issue with no worries about medical underwriting. These situations include:

- Some states allow consumers to buy another type of Medigap policy called Medicare SELECT. Those who purchase Medicare SELECT have the right to change their minds up to 12 months after purchase, during which time they can switch to a standard Medigap policy.

- Individuals with end-stage renal disease (ESRD) may not be able to buy a Medigap policy until they turn 65, or they may be able to purchase one—just not the one they want since federal law doesn't require insurance companies to sell Medigap policies to people under 65. Please see pages 74 and 75 for states that require Medigap policies for those under 65.

- Individuals with group health coverage through an employer, union or spouse's employer are already covered and may not want to enroll in Part B. However, should their coverage end, they will get a chance to enroll in Part B without incurring the late enrollment penalty. Therefore, their Medigap open enrollment period starts at that point. If an individual chooses to enroll in Part B while they still have employer coverage or union coverage, their open enrollment period begins at that time. If they neglect to purchase a Medigap policy at the same time, they will miss their open enrollment.

- You may have a guaranteed issue right. Please see an explanation of this on page 76.

Navigating Through Medicare

These states require insurance companies to offer at least one kind of Medigap policy to people with Medicare under 65:

California*	Maryland	Oklahoma
Colorado	Massachusetts**	Oregon
Connecticut	Michigan	Pennsylvania
Delaware**	Minnesota	South Dakota
Florida	Mississippi	Tennessee

Navigating Through Medicare

Georgia	Missouri	Texas
Hawaii	New Hampshire	Oklahoma
Illinois	New Jersey	Vermont*
Louisiana	New York	Wisconsin
Maine	North Carolina	

*A Medigap policy isn't available to people with ESRD under 65. **A Medigap policy is only available to people with ESRD.

If you're already enrolled in Medicare Part B, you'll get a Medigap open enrollment period when you turn 65. You'll probably have a wider choice of Medigap policies and be able to get a lower premium at that time. Even if you don't live in any of these states, some insurance companies may voluntarily sell Medigap policies to people under 65, although they will probably cost you more than Medigap policies sold to people over 65, and they can use medical underwriting. Check with your state about what rights you may have under state law. For state requirements, call your State Health Insurance Assistance Program (SHIP).

73

Understanding Guaranteed Issue Rights

Guaranteed issue rights (sometimes called *Medigap protections*) are situations in which insurance companies are required to sell or offer you a Medigap policy even if you have health problems and are not in your personal open enrollment period. Additionally, they cannot offer any preexisting condition exclusions nor can they increase your premium based on your health.

In many cases, you have a guaranteed issue right when your other health coverage has changed in some way. This can occur, for instance, when you lose or drop an employer's coverage.

You may also have what's called a "trial right." This allows you the opportunity to try a Medicare Advantage plan and still buy a Medigap policy if you change your mind. As long as this occurs within a set period of time, you can get a guaranteed issue Medigap policy.

To secure your rights, make sure you keep the following for proof of compliance:

- A copy of any letters, notices and claim denials as proof of coverage
- Anything from the insurer with your name on it
- The postmarked envelope these papers come in as proof of when your Medicare Advantage plan was mailed.

It's always best to apply for a Medigap policy **before** your current health coverage ends, so you can ensure you have no breaks in coverage. When you apply, set the policy's start date as the date your existing coverage is slated to end.

The guaranteed issue rights mentioned on the previous page are from federal law. It's important to remember many states also provide additional Medicare rights you may qualify for when the previous circumstances don't apply. Call your state health insurance assistance program (SHIP) or state insurance department for more information. You may even find that both federal and state guarantees apply. Should this occur, choose the rights that give you the best choices and coverage options, or check out Medicare.gov.

Navigating Through Medicare

Your Guaranteed Issue Rights

An insurance company can't refuse to sell you a Medigap policy under the following situations:

Guaranteed Issue Right Situation	You Have the Right to Buy	When to Apply for a Medigap Policy
1: You're in a Medicare Advantage plan, and: - It is leaving Medicare - It stops giving care in your area - You move out of the plan's service area	Medigap Plan A, B, C, F, K, L, M or N sold in your state by any insurance company. You only have this right if you switch to original Medicare rather than join another Medicare Advantage plan.	As early as 60 calendar days before the date your healthcare coverage ends, but no later than 63 calendar days after your healthcare coverage ends. Medigap coverage can't start until your Medicare Advantage plan coverage ends.

Navigating Through Medicare

2: You have original Medicare and an employer group health plan (including retiree or COBRA coverage) or union coverage that pays after Medicare pays and that plan is ending. **Note:** In this situation, you may have additional rights under state law.	Medigap Plan A, B, C, F, K or L sold in your state by any insurance company. --- If you have COBRA coverage, you can either buy a Medigap policy right away or wait until the COBRA coverage ends.	No later than 63 calendar days after the latest of these three dates: • Date the coverage ends • Date on the notice you get telling you the coverage is ending (if you get one) • Date on a claim denial, if this is the only way you know your coverage ended
3: You have original Medicare and a Medicare SELECT policy. You move out of the Medicare SELECT policy's service area. --- You can keep your Medigap policy, or you may switch to another one.	Medigap Plan A, B, C, F, K or L sold by any insurance company in your state or the state you are moving to.	As early as 60 calendar days before the date your healthcare coverage will end, but no later than 63 calendar days after your healthcare coverage ends.

Navigating Through Medicare

4: (Trial Right) You joined a Medicare Advantage plan or Programs of All-Inclusive Care for the Elderly (PACE) when you were first eligible for Medicare Part A at 65, and within the first year of joining, you decide to switch to original Medicare.	Any Medigap policy sold in your state by any insurance company.	As early as 60 calendar days before the date your coverage ends, but no later than 63 calendar days after your coverage ends. **Note:** Your rights may last for an extra 12 months under certain circumstances.
5: (Trial Right) You dropped a Medigap policy to join a Medicare Advantage plan (or to switch to a Medicare SELECT policy) for the first time; you have been in the plan less than a year, and want to switch back.	The Medigap policy you had before you joined the Medicare Advantage plan or Medicare SELECT policy, if the same insurance company you had before still sells it. If your former Medigap policy isn't available, you can buy a Medigap plan A, B, C, F, K or L sold in your state by any insurer.	As early as 60 calendar days before the date your coverage ends, but no later than 63 calendar days after your coverage ends. **Note:** Your rights may last for an extra 12 months under certain circumstances.

Navigating Through Medicare

6: Your Medigap insurance company goes bankrupt and you lose your coverage, or your Medigap policy coverage otherwise ends through no fault of your own.	Medigap Plan A, B, C, F, K or L sold in your state by any insurance company.	No later than 63 calendar days from the date your coverage ends.
7: You leave a Medicare Advantage plan or drop a Medigap policy because the company hasn't followed the rules or misled you.	Medigap Plan A, B, C, F, K or L sold in your state by any insurance company.	No later than 63 calendar days from the date your coverage ends.

Chapter 4: Budgeting for Medicare

No matter what plan you select, you will have some combination of premiums, deductibles, copayments and other expenses to deal with—as if being retired and living on a fixed income weren't difficult enough. Then, there is always the prescription drug donut hole you may fall into and should be prepared to deal with financially.

Luckily, steps can be taken to better fit these expenses into your restricted, postretirement budget.

Look at the Numbers and Assume the Worst

The first step in creating or revising a postretirement budget to fit in Medicare and medical costs is to add up your average monthly expenses based on your actual spending history over the last six to 12 months. Use your bank and credit card statements to identify that amount. Remember, too, that items you routinely put on credit cards count as expenses—it's not just the credit card payment that does.

Next, determine the maximum amount of medical expenses you face based on your plan's deductibles, premiums and copayments. For example, if you choose the High-Deductible Plan

F with a $2,100 deductible. In this exercise you would assume you will end up spending the entire deductible in a year. This can be different with a Medicare Advantage plan because they have a maximum out-of-pocket expense, which may be quite a bit higher than any Medigap deductible.

- Add the total deductible and estimated copayments (based on how often you generally visit your primary care physician and any specialists). Divide this by 12 to get your monthly amount.
- Add the monthly premium to this total.
- Subtract your monthly Social Security income from this total.
- Take the remaining amount and divide your retirement account balances by that number to estimate how many months or years your current retirement savings will support your present spending and potential Medicare spending.

Making Adjustments

If your current spending and anticipated medical expenses, based on a worst-case scenario, is high enough to deplete your savings balances before you've lived out your total life expectancy or if it's simply too close for comfort, you must take another look at your budget and trim your expenses.

You never want to underestimate the amount of medical spending you will have in a year. So, when adjusting your budget, do not tweak that amount. Instead, look at the various items you spend money on each month and highlight, or circle, those you can reduce or eliminate.

For some, this may mean making simple reductions such as keeping cable but terminating some of the expensive added channels and features, or buying store-brand grocery items. For others with a tighter budget, it may mean getting rid of cable and other luxuries altogether.

Finding Balance

Retirement is a very challenging segment of life because, for the first time, you have total control over how each of your days is spent. With that control, you may have certain activities that are extremely important to your physical and mental health as well as your emotional status.

When cutting your budget to accommodate the limits of Social Security income and your savings, you must ensure you find a way to balance these cuts with retaining access to activities and places important to you.

For some seniors, a consistent social presence is very important, and very difficult to maintain without memberships to clubs and social groups. If this is true for you, you may need to find a way to keep an activity in the budget, or substitute it with something less expensive. For example, you may find you are able to replace a special fee-only club membership with participation in a free book club at your local library. Or, if the other people involved in the paid club are important to your happiness, you may need to organize alternative events to keep in contact with them.

Finding balance isn't always easy, but it is important you do not discount how vital certain activities are to your overall happiness, and do not allow that happiness to be sacrificed for your budget.

Developing Alternatives

It's always a good to have several different versions of your budget so you can shift gears quickly as the need arises. I suggest having three budgets. The first is your ideal budget with few sacrifices. This is the one you hope to be able to support throughout your retirement. It includes most, if not all, of the expenses you want and enjoy but is still reasonable considering your savings and Social Security income.

The second budget should be a step-down version with some sacrifices. Within this budget should still be a moderate level of fun and unnecessary spending.

The third budget should be your most stripped-down version. It should be considered your emergency budget and is the one you would put in place should you face some sort of financial catastrophe, such as a loss in your savings or a very large, unexpected bill.

Chapter 5: Frequently Asked Questions

After reading this book, you should have a much better understanding of how the Medicare system and all its parts work. However, you may have found this information created almost as many questions as it answered. That's a good thing—because it means your understanding has grown enough that you have a whole new group of questions. On the following pages you'll find a list of the questions we're asked the most. Hopefully you'll find the answers you need there. If not, give us a call.

Q: After signing up for Medicare and a Medigap or Medicare Advantage plan, will I be able to visit the same physicians and facilities?

Many, many doctors and facilities accept Medicare patients and, if your existing physicians do, then you can continue to see them. However, some doctors limit the number of Medicare recipients they treat, so check with your physicians in advance.

Q: After signing up, how much will I have to pay to visit my doctor or get treatment in a hospital?

This answer depends heavily on the plan you select. Medicare Advantage plans have copayments and co-insurance requirements and yours could be very different from someone else's. If you have Medicare Supplement Plan F, then you will have only the premium expense each month and no out-of-pocket copayments. If you have the High-Deductible Plan F, then you may have to pay out-of-pocket expenses until you've reached the deductible limit. If you enrolled during general open enrollment, had a preexisting condition excluded for a certain period, and your visit pertains to that condition, you may not have any coverage at all and need to pay the entire cost of the visit out of your own pocket. Carefully read your plan documents so you understand in advance what your charges could be. If you have questions, call your plan provider.

Q: Will my prescription medications be covered as is or will they change?

If you purchase a Medicare supplement, you need a separate prescription plan. Medicare Advantage, on the other hand, generally includes prescription coverage, but it's not a guarantee. Look at the policy benefits before purchasing to make sure it does.

As far as maintaining the same medications, this could vary. You can go to the Medicare.gov website and enter the prescriptions you take as well as your zip code. Then, you will be able to see which plans cover your current meds. This, however, is not a guarantee of coverage. To dig deeper, you may want to request a copy of the plan's formulary to see their specific list of covered medications.

Q: Will Medicare cover my flu and shingles shots?

Due to the prevalence of shingles in people over age 65, most drug plans include the vaccine in their formulary. You should check with your plan or any plans you consider, before signing on with them. You can also ask the pharmacy or facility where you get the flu shot whether Medicare covers it.

Medicare Part B may not cover the shingles vaccine, but it *does* cover vaccines for the flu, swine flu and pneumonia. Finally, if you are at medium to high risk for contracting hepatitis B, then you may be entitled to a vaccine under Part B.

Q: Will Medicare cover dental, vision or hearing treatment or check-ups?

Medigap policies will not generally cover extra services such as hearing, dental and vision. Medicare itself does not cover these, either, unless it's medically necessary (such as cataracts), in which case Medicare and your Supplement should cover it. Many Medicare Advantage plans include limited coverage for these services while also including prescription drug coverage.

Q: How can I avoid the so-called donut hole (aka Medicare Prescription Gap)?

While the prescription donut hole has a higher trigger than it once had, the gap has not disappeared and is not something you can generally avoid.

The way the donut hole works is after you pay your prescription deductible, and your drug plan pays its total responsibility for the initial 100 percent covered portion ($2,970 for 2013), you are responsible for paying the full cost of your generic prescriptions and 50 percent of your name-brand drugs. This responsibility continues until you've spent a total of $4,750 out of pocket, at which point your drug plan once again pays for most of the costs.

The more generic drugs you get, the less your drug plan will spend and the longer you can delay reaching the gap. Also, pay attention to what different pharmacies charge for various generics. Some offer them at a fixed price of $5 per refill. Lastly, you can talk to your doctor about getting samples and discount coupons.

Q: What happens if I have an accident or catastrophic illness away from home?

If you have Medicare Advantage, you can get coverage for an emergency anywhere in the U.S. You cannot, however, get routine or follow-up care away from home.

If you have Plan F or Plan G, you can go anywhere in the U.S. for any kind of treatment, as long as the facility or practitioner you visit accepts Medicare.

Q: I plan to move soon. Will I be able to switch Medicare Advantage plans or will I be forced to keep the same plan?

As long as a plan is not offered in the area you are moving to, you are permitted to switch plans and carriers. If they have the plan in the new area, you are not eligible to switch.

If you've found yourself unhappy with the service and coverage of your existing Medicare Advantage plan, a move may offer a great opportunity to rectify that by signing up for the plan that offers the coverage and options you want.

Q: How much should I expect to pay for a Medicare supplement or Advantage plan?

First, you'll have the Part B premium since you must pay for Part B to get a Medicare supplement plan (Medigap).

Your Medicare Advantage plan premiums could cost nothing or hundreds per month. It's up to you how much you pay. Your premium is determined by the plan you choose and the features it offers. Premiums are not locked in and you may experience increases from year to year.

A Medigap plan generally costs $100 to $300 per month.

In addition to the Plan B and Medigap premiums, you may need to pay copayments, deductibles and/or coinsurance.

Copayments are small fees you pay when you visit a doctor or treatment facility. They should be listed in your policy, which makes them very predictable and easy to budget.

A deductible is the out-of-pocket amount you must initially pay before your plan begins supporting any of the expenses. High deductibles help you design a plan with low premiums but can create a hefty financial responsibility should you need treatment.

Coinsurance payments are the amount of the total cost of a treatment or procedure you must pay over and above your deductible and copayment. Coinsurance payments are usually a percentage of the total cost above those benchmarks.

Q: What will my Part A premium cost?

Premiums for Medicare can change annually, so you should always double-check to get the most up-to-date information. In 2013, the Part A premium was premium-free for most seniors over age 65.

Q: What should I expect for Part A deductibles?

Deductibles for Part A can vary. For example, an individual staying in a hospital for treatment may pay as much as $1,184 for the visit during a single benefit period. Therefore, when you are released, if you have no more inpatient treatment or skilled nursing facility treatment for 60 days and are admitted once again, you must pay the $1,184 deductible once more. Depending on your Medigap plan, this may be covered 100 percent.

Q: What will be my Part B premium and deductibles?

The Part B premium varies depending on your taxable income from the tax year two years prior to the current year. In 2014, taxable income from 2012 was the basis for premiums. If an individual filing single made $85,000 or less in 2012 ($170,000 for joint filers), their monthly premium would be $104.90; individuals who made $214,001 or more and couples who made more than $428,000 had monthly premiums of $335.70.

The Part B deductible is much simpler to determine because it is a flat amount no matter what your income is. In 2013, the Part B deductible was $147 per year.

Q: What will be my Part D premium and deductibles?

Part D, your prescription drug coverage, can vary by plan. It can be affected by your Modified Adjusted Gross Income (MAGI), although this income limit affects just 5 percent of the high-income seniors covered by Medicare.

The deductible for Plan D also varies. In 2013, the deductible could not exceed $325. Plans may also have a copayment and coinsurance amount.

An additional cost in Plan D is the coverage gap or donut hole. In 2013, the hole began once you and your plan spent a combined $2,970. At that point, you received a discount on drugs but were required to pay any amount due after the discount was applied. This responsibility continues until your out-of-pocket expenses reached $4,750. At this point, your drug plan once again paid for most of the costs.

Finally, if you enroll late, you may be charged a penalty. This penalty may stick with you for the rest of your life, so it's important to monitor you reenrollment dates carefully.

Q: How much can I expect my Medicare Supplement premium to increase each year?

Unfortunately, this is an impossible question to answer. The amount of increase can depend on the plan itself, the claims experience of the group of policyholders—meaning the actual claims put through by the covered group—and, in some cases, the number of claims you have had. You may find an increase with a particular company is based on your attained age, or even changes to Medicare itself.

These changes may make it in your best interest to get rates for a new policy every few years. Just because you chose the most competitively priced policy starting out doesn't mean it will maintain a competitive premium. Think of it as you would any other insurance policy, such as auto or home—you must compare prices often to make sure you get the best deal.

Q: Will my preexisting health conditions have an effect on my policy?

This depends on when you enroll in your Medigap Plan.

Enrolling during your open enrollment period ensures your policy is a guaranteed issue for any condition. You will have no preexisting condition exclusion, and your policy's price cannot be based on your health prior to the policy's issue.

If you enroll after your initial personal open enrollment period, which occurs during the six months after you enroll and are accepted into the Medicare program, your application can be denied based solely on your preexisting health conditions.

Q: Although I'm retired and no longer working, I still have health insurance through my former employer or union. This coverage doesn't just protect me but also extends to my spouse. Should I still enroll in Part B?

As with many questions related to Medicare, your position may be too unique for a generic answer. However, generally speaking, when you become eligible for Medicare, you need to enroll in both Part A and Part B to get all the benefits included in your retiree plan. Your retiree plan may offer benefits that fill in Medicare's gaps of coverage and may include extra benefits such as prescription drugs. Your retiree plan is not a Medigap policy, thus generally you will still need to enroll in Part A and B. Talk to your plan administrator if you are not certain how your retiree coverage works and which benefits your plan includes.

When you turn 65, even if you are covered by an employer or union, you will be automatically enrolled in Part B unless you opt out. Opting out can create a penalty if your employer health insurance is not considered creditable coverage, so make sure you verify this before you do anything.

You should enroll in a plan during your open enrollment so you can get the best rates and ensure the underwriting is not based on any preexisting conditions.

Q: I am retired and do not have coverage through a former employer or union, but I am covered by my spouse's current employer. Should I still enroll in Part B or opt out?

As mentioned in the last answer, a retiree plan is not a Medigap policy, thus the need to enroll in Part A and B. You need to verify you have creditable coverage through your spouse's plan to opt out and avoid any preexisting condition exclusions. If you can verify your coverage is creditable, then you can opt out of Part B.

Q: Which plan is the best?

I love when people ask me this question because I can give them an answer that really makes their day. Plans F and G are my favorites. They have the most benefits and there are no surprises hidden within. Both are straightforward plans with no medical approval necessary if you enroll during your open enrollment. The out-of-pocket cost is little to nothing, which makes them very affordable and manageable. If you prefer, you can choose the High-Deductible Plan F, which allows for a lower premium, although this can come back to bite you should you need treatment and have to pay the high deductible. With careful planning, however, you can often control these costs and may find it fits better in your budget.

I also suggest Plan G to those who are in very good health. This plan requires medical underwriting, so if you are not in very good health, you may be turned down. However, for those in tip-top shape, this plan can be less expensive and have lower yearly premium increases since, thanks to the medical underwriting, the claims going to the insurer are generally predictable and small.

Finally, Plan N offers another option for a low premium and high deductible. This plan also has copayments, which further reduce premiums by putting more of the financial responsibility on the insured. In certain states, excess charges from any nonparticipating physicians are also shifted onto you, but are capped at 15 percent of the Medicare payment.

Q: Can I have the Medicare Supplement and Part D all in one policy?

Medigap policies sold after January 1, 2006, are not allowed to include prescription drug coverage, so you must get that coverage separately. Alternatively, many Medicare Advantage plans offer prescription drug benefits, so you might choose that option instead, if having everything in one plan is important to you.

Q: Why not go with an Advantage plan instead since they have lower monthly premiums?

Ultimately, while your budget will definitely be a factor in the Medigap or Medicare Advantage plan you select, the price of the premium should not be your only consideration. Premiums can be deceptive; a plan with a very low premium might have a very high deductible and a very high out-of-pocket maximum or offer fewer benefits than you need. A plan with a high premium may offer more savings as it may provide coverage for those things that concern and affect you.

Additionally, a plan with a high premium may not have the same out-of-pocket deductible as a plan with a lower premium. This can result in a more budget-friendly, predictable experience and in the long run, be easier to afford.

Q: What does each plan cover?

There are a number of coverage options among all the available plans. Some deal with actual treatments and services covered while others deal with the out-of-pocket costs you can expect. Please refer to the tables beginning on page 38 for details on each plan.

Chapter 6: Glossary

You may notice when researching your Medicare options and going through various written material, a lot of jargon is used to lay out the various aspects and points of each plan and option. In this section, you will find a breakdown of many of the terms you see. This will make it easier for you to move forward and make the necessary decisions to ensure a successful transition into Medicare coverage.

DEFINITIONS

Ambulatory surgical center: A facility where simpler surgeries are performed for patients who are not expected to need more than 24 hours of care.

Appeal: An appeal is the action you can take if you disagree with a coverage or payment decision made by Medicare, your Medicare health plan, or your Medicare prescription drug plan. You can appeal if Medicare or your plan denies one of the following:

1. A healthcare service, supply or prescription you think you should be able to get but are being denied

2. Healthcare, supplies or a prescription drug you already received

3. A change in the amount you must pay for a prescription drug

You can also appeal if you already get coverage and Medicare or your plan stops paying.

Assignment: An agreement by your doctor or other healthcare provider or supplier to be paid directly by Medicare, to accept the payment amount Medicare approves for the service and not to bill you for any more than the Medicare deductible and coinsurance.

Benefit period: The way original Medicare measures your use of hospital and skilled nursing facility (SNF) services. A benefit period begins the day you go into a hospital or skilled nursing facility. The benefit period ends when you have not received any inpatient hospital care (or skilled care in a SNF) for 60 days in a row. If you go into a hospital or a skilled nursing facility after one benefit period has ended, a new benefit period begins. You must pay the inpatient hospital deductible for each benefit period. There is no limit to the number of benefit periods.

Coinsurance: Amounts you may be required to pay as your share of the cost for services after you pay any deductibles. Coinsurance is usually a percentage (for example, 20 percent).

Copayment: An amount you may be required to pay as your share of the cost for a medical service or supply, such as a doctor's visit, hospital outpatient visit or a prescription. A copayment is usually a set amount, rather than a percentage. For example, you might pay $10 or $20 for a doctor's visit or prescription. Copayments can go toward deductible totals.

Creditable coverage: Previous health insurance coverage that can be used to shorten a preexisting condition waiting period under a Medigap policy. To be considered creditable, the coverage must pay at least the same in benefits as Medicare.

Creditable prescription drug coverage: Prescription drug coverage (for instance, from an employer or union) that is expected to pay, on average, as much as Medicare's standard prescription drug coverage. People who have this kind of coverage when they become eligible for Medicare can generally keep it and not be required to pay a penalty if they decide to enroll in a Medicare prescription drug coverage plan later.

Critical access hospital: A small facility that provides outpatient services as well as inpatient services on a limited basis to people in rural areas and is designated as a critical access hospital by Medicare.

Custodial care: Nonskilled personal care, such as help with activities of daily living such as bathing, dressing, eating, getting in or out of a bed or chair, moving around and using the bathroom. It may also include the kind of health-related care most people do themselves, such as using eye drops. In most cases, Medicare does not pay for custodial care as it is considered nonmedical.

Deductible: The amount you must pay for healthcare or prescriptions before original Medicare, your prescription drug plan or your other insurance begins to pay.

Disabled: An injury or illness that prevents an individual from performing the ordinary duties of any position, potentially lasting at least one year or possibly resulting in the death of the individual.

Durable medical equipment: Certain medical equipment, such as a walker, wheelchair or hospital bed, ordered by your doctor for use in the home.

Elimination periods: The time period between an injury and the receipt of benefit payments.

End-stage renal disease (ESRD): Permanent kidney failure that requires a regular course of dialysis or a kidney transplant.

Extra Help: A Medicare program to help people with limited income and resources pay Medicare prescription drug program costs, such as premiums, deductibles and coinsurance. To find out about Extra Help options and apply for assistance, visit *www.ssa.gov/prescription**help**/*.

Formulary: A list of prescription drugs covered by a prescription drug plan or another insurance plan offering prescription drug benefits.

Free look: The number of days an insured is allowed to review a new policy to decide whether to keep it. Policies terminated during their free-look period have no penalties.

Home healthcare: Healthcare services and supplies a doctor determines you may receive in your home under a plan of care established by your doctor. Medicare only covers home healthcare on a limited basis as ordered by your doctor.

Hospice: A special way of caring for people who are terminally ill. Hospice care involves a team-oriented approach addressing the medical, physical, social, emotional and spiritual needs of the patient. Hospice also provides support to the patient's family or caregiver.

Inpatient: An individual who is admitted into a hospital. It includes at least one night of care, but an overnight stay in a hospital does not, in itself, mean one has been admitted or is an inpatient.

Inpatient rehabilitation facility: A hospital or part of a hospital that provides an intensive rehabilitation program to inpatients.

Institution: A facility that provides short- or long-term care, such as a nursing home, skilled nursing facility (SNF) or other rehabilitation hospital. Private residences, such as an assisted living facility or group home are not considered institutions for Medicare purposes.

Lifetime reserve days: In original Medicare, these are additional days Medicare will pay for when you are in a hospital for more than 90 days. You have a total of 60 reserve days that can be used during your lifetime. For each lifetime reserve day, Medicare pays all covered costs except for a daily coinsurance ($608 in 2014). (Medigap Plan F will pay this deductible.)

Long-term care: A variety of services that help people with their medical and nonmedical needs over a period of time. Long-term care can be provided at home, in the community or in various types of facilities, including nursing homes and assisted living facilities. Most long-term care is custodial care and nonmedical. Medicare does not pay for this type of care if this is the only kind of care you need.

Long-term care hospital: Acute care hospitals that provide treatment for patients who stay, on average, more than 25 days. Most patients are transferred from an intensive or critical care unit. Services provided include comprehensive rehabilitation, respiratory therapy, head trauma treatment and pain management.

Medically necessary: Services or supplies needed for the diagnosis or treatment of your medical condition and meet accepted standards of medical practice.

Medicare-approved amount: In original Medicare, it is the amount a doctor or supplier who accepts assignment can be paid. It includes what Medicare pays and any deductible, coinsurance or copayment you pay. It may be less than the actual amount a doctor or supplier normally charges.

Medicare health plan: A Medicare health plan is offered by a private company contracted with Medicare to provide Medicare Part A and Part B benefits to people with Medicare who enroll in the plan. This term is used throughout this booklet to include all Medicare Advantage plans, Medicare Cost plans, Demonstration/Pilot Programs, and Programs of All-inclusive Care for the Elderly (PACE). Medigap plans are not included.

Medicare plan: Refers to any way, other than original Medicare, that you can get your Medicare health or prescription drug coverage. It includes all Medicare health plans and Medicare prescription drug plans.

Network: A group of treatment facilities or practitioners who have agreed to provide members of certain Medicare plans with services and supplies at a discounted price.

Nonparticipating: Physicians and facilities that do not accept Medicare for payment of services.

Out-of-pocket costs: Health or prescription drug costs you must pay on your own because Medicare or other insurance does not cover them.

Outpatient: A patient who received treatment but whose doctor has not written an order to admit them into the hospital. Outpatients can stay overnight and not be admitted.

Participating: Medical treatment facilities and service providers who accept Medicare payments for services rendered.

Preexisting condition: A health condition or problem you had prior to the date a new insurance policy starts.

Premium: The periodic payment to Medicare, an insurance company or a healthcare plan for health or prescription drug coverage.

Preventive services: Healthcare to prevent illness or detect illness at an early stage, when treatment is likely to work best (for example, Pap tests, flu shots and mammograms).

Prodrug: An oral form of a drug that when ingested breaks down into the same active ingredient found in the injectable form of the drug.

Quality Improvement Organization: A group of practicing doctors and other healthcare experts paid by the federal government to check and improve the care given to people with Medicare.

Prescription drug plan (Medicare Part D): A standalone drug plan that adds prescription drug coverage to original Medicare, some Medicare Cost plans, some Medicare Private-Fee-for-Service plans, and Medicare Medical Savings Account plans. These plans are offered by insurance companies and other private companies approved by Medicare. Medicare Advantage plans may also offer prescription drug coverage following the same rules as Medicare prescription drug plans.

Referral: A written order from your primary care doctor for you to see a specialist or get certain medical services. In many Health

Maintenance Organizations (HMOs), you need a referral before getting medical care from anyone except your primary care doctor. If you do not get a referral first, the plan may not pay for the services. Referrals are never needed for Medigap policies.

Religious nonmedical healthcare institution (RNHCI): A facility that provides nonmedical healthcare items and services to people who need hospital or skilled nursing facility care, but for whom the care would be inconsistent with their religious beliefs.

Service area: A geographic area where a health insurance plan accepts members if it limits membership based on where people live. For plans that limit which doctors and hospital you may use, it is also generally the area where you can get routine (nonemergency) services. The plan may disenroll you if you move out of the plan's service area.

Skilled nursing facility care: Skilled nursing care and rehabilitation services provided on a continuous, daily basis in a skilled nursing facility. Examples of skilled nursing facility care include physical therapy or intravenous injections that can only be given by a registered nurse or doctor.

TTY: A teletypewriter is a communication device used by people who are deaf, hard-of-hearing or have severe speech impairment. People who do not have a TTY can communicate with a TTY user through a message relay center. An MRC has operators available to send and interpret TTY messages.

Waiting period: The period of time between the need for medical attention or treatment and the date on which policy benefits begin to pay out.

www.ingramcontent.com/pod-product-compliance
Lightning Source LLC
Chambersburg PA
CBHW051730170526
45167CB00002B/874